CW00832489

Never Still
Nivver Still

A narrative poem
by Joan Lennon

Translated into Fair Isle dialect
by Anne Sinclair

Illustrated by Lucy Wheeler

Published by
Hansel Cooperative Press
www.hanselcooperativepress.co.uk

Text by: Joan Lennon, translated into Fair Isle dialect
by Anne Sinclair

© Published in 2022 by Hansel Co-operative Press

ISBN: 978-0-9932242-4-9

Hansel is a non-profit-making co-operative which promotes
literary and artistic works relating to Shetland and Orkney.

Hansel Co-operative Press,
Rockville,
Nibon,
Hamar,
Shetland,
ZE2 9RQ
www.hanselcooperativepress.co.uk

Text: © Joan Lennon and Anne Sinclair

Illustration and design: © Lucy Wheeler

Editor: Jim Mainland

Printed by: Route 1 Print
www.route1print.co.uk

Sea levels source:
©www.floodmap.net data

www.hanselcooperativepress.co.uk

The Never Still Story

It was the year of applying. I'd been working with students at Dundee University as an RLF Fellow for the past three years – deeply satisfying work but it meant that whenever I saw any opportunities for writing retreats, they were only things to ogle and dream over. I couldn't take the time to make a stab at going. But then my contract ended.

'New beginnings!' I cried. 'New writing in new places!'

But first ...

Writing a proposal is a lot like putting in an offer on a house. You have to commit. You have to be able to see yourself in that specific place, sitting at that exact table, being inspired by the view out of that particular window. You have to really, really care. And each project has to be fine-tuned to the place, the length of time, the level of prestige. There are clues in the way the offer is worded and who has been selected in previous years. Somehow, through your words, you have to convince the selectors that you, of all the eager applicants, are the one who best fits *their* idea of the writer who should be sitting at that table, fingers poised and ready to produce greatness.

It's hard work, applying, and the success rate is low. It's quite like the success rate cheetahs experience when hunting. But if you don't put everything you've got into it, you, like the cheetah, will limp away with nothing.

I have a lot of sympathy for cheetahs.

I started to apply. Though each project and place was different, I at least knew what direction I wanted to be heading in. Narrative poetry. I write poetry – I write prose – and narrative poetry is one of the places where the two meet. It's a form that I have worked with a number of times in my writing life, and it has deep satisfactions.

Then, in the course of trawling for opportunities, I came across the Fair Isle Studio Creative Residencies. A winter month in a little blue cottage on Scotland's most remote inhabited island ... Robert Louis Stevenson might famously have said of Fair Isle that 'It is a conspicuous example of matter in the wrong place' but I was happy to go and prove him wrong. (He also wrote to his mother that the Fair Isle coast was 'the wildest and most unpitying that we have yet seen' and that was in June!)

I'd been to mainland Shetland back in 2013 as part of the Farlin Project, a joint initiative pairing makers and poets from Fife and from Shetland. I worked with Sarah Riley, a textile artist, on a series of poems about hands, to which she responded in a number of pieces in latex. It was a fascinating collaboration, and Shetland as a place completely seduced me. Sarah also translated the poems into the dialect of Burra, some of it in collaboration with her mum and aunties, sitting round the kitchen table. And we made a recording of our two voices reading the two versions.

I knew I wanted a Fair Isle project to have those elements of collaboration too – translation, art, sound. As for my part, the shape was there from the start: three narrative poems, telling the stories of three women's experiences of Fair Isle in three distinctly different time periods, inter-leaved with descriptive poems about the way the natural world was constantly changing. In geological time, Fair Isle has travelled from the South Pole, been part of and then split away from North America, been engulfed and scoured by glaciers, and surrounded by sea. Now it is midway between the Orkney and Shetland archipelagos, where the Atlantic and the North Sea meet. But physical change has not stopped. The wind and the water con-tinue to carve and shape the Isle – the northern Raevas gloup fell in in 1916, and a new geo was formed as recently as 1967 when part of the coastline collapsed – and rising sea levels and the dissipation of milder ocean currents due to climate change will continue to have an impact on its existence – and the lives of its inhabitants - in the future.

At the beginning, I thought of the three stories I wanted to tell as being called Coming, Going, and Staying. The Isle is a small place, 3½ miles long by 1½ miles wide, with finite resources. Throughout its history, when the population gets too large, some have had to leave if they are to thrive or even survive. When the population gets too small, life becomes less and less viable, and new folk are, as they are now, desperately needed.

Fair Isle and its people are never still.

So, I wrote my proposal, sent it off with the others, and waited. There were lots of no's and then, delightfully and unexpectedly, there was a yes. For the month of February 2020, the Fair Isle Studio, Lower Leogh, was to be mine. I began to prepare with more research, buying wet weather gear, engaging in a lot of imagining, speculation, and a fair wack of worry.

And the project began to grow.

I was going to be writing about worlds that were physically, historically and linguistically grounded in reality, but I was not writing as a historian, a scientist or a linguist. Just as narrative poetry is a place where poetry and prose meet, and Fair Isle is a place where land, sea and air meet, the experiences of my characters were going to be of where the mundane and the strange or other-worldly meet. I didn't want this to be too explicit. The third character, for example, isn't explicitly a selkie. The second character isn't explicitly a witch. The first character is a Finn, a person in whom story and song meet, who is a go-between for the human and the spirit world. I used the word 'trow' instead of 'troll', to suggest not the angry, stupid, revolting creature that is the version Christianity allowed to survive, but the idea of the Goodfolk. Still dangerous – still chancy – but also connected to the humans who shared the Isle through their passion for music and story and song.

Many of the ways my characters revealed themselves to me was through words and concepts that are specific to the Isle. I grew to understand the second character, for example, through learning that a gamfer is a ghost you might meet in the mist – that mareel is the name for the blue phosphorescence microscopic marine animals pro- duce from time to time near the shore – that 'cold iron' is what you say to ward off the bad luck that comes from having a woman on a boat. By knowing that these things were givens in her world, I got to know her better. I could see her more clearly.

But how to make her as clear to others?

I asked a group of writing friends, 'Can you make a poem out of just sounds, without the reader knowing the meaning?' and sent them this:

Roosts, noosts
yoals and yows
kishies and krubs
baas, geos and kletts
voar and hairst *

They let me get away with it, but when it came to becom- ing part of Never Still, words like these and others not in common use in other parts of the world began to cause problems. Without the sense, isn't the reader jolted out of the story? And what about words that are not exclusively Fair Isle, or exclusively Shetlandic, but just Scottish, like croft or lochan or skirl or dyke? Will a non-Scottish reader know that a croft is a smallholding and a lochan is a small lake, a skirl is a shrill cry and a dyke is a wall? That a smoored fire is one that has been banked up for the night, and a kirkyard is a cemetery? Which words would be clear from context, and which would just be jarring gibberish?

And what about technical terms? Before working on this poem, I knew about the importance of kelp forests in sequestering carbon dioxide, but I didn't know that the stem of a kelp was called a stipe or that, instead of roots, they had holdfasts. Maybe my reader didn't either.

But the three sections, though long for poems, are short for stories, and if I was going to draw my readers in – get them to become part of the process – I couldn't afford to keep knocking them out of these worlds to check out a footnote or flip to the back of the book for a glossary. Stop and start is a killer for rhythm.

Then, when I handed the poem over to Anne to translate into the Fair Isle dialect, there were new things to wrestle with. Sometimes it was the cry, 'We just wouldn't say that!' or even, 'Your writing is so English!' Sometimes there is simply no Fair Isle dialect word for something, like, for example, 'tree'. Then all she could do was put the English in instead. But there were also times when, instead of no word, there were *multiple* words. Where I had written 'shore' or 'wave' or 'cliff', she had to ask me what *kind* of shore or wave or cliff did I mean? There are no generic terms for such things – only specific words for particular sorts of shores or waves or cliffs. The moder dy, for example, the landward tending swell used by fishermen as a guide, or bummlie, the lumpy waves which make the boat rock, or rank for a tide rip.

In this tiny place, exact language could mean you didn't die.

As it happened, I only met Anne near the end of my time on Fair Isle, when she took me round the George Waterston Museum. It was a visit that had been put off a few times because the wind needed to either drop or come from another direction if she was to safely open the museum door. Some of the multitude of fascinating things I learned then found their way into the poem. Others I garnered over excellent coffee at her kitchen table. I made notes, more and more frantically as the last days slipped away.

I flew home from Fair Isle on a beautiful clear day, and straight into the arms of the pandemic. Like many, for weeks after I couldn't write or read. My memories of February became first blurry, then implausible, then began to disappear. The turnaround was just as gradual.

10

I started corresponding with Anne, which became a weekly phone chat, which became a Fair Isle lifeline. And the shamble of notes and snippets slowly became my part of this book. The rest is Anne's, of course, and Lucy's, who brought her artist's eye and skills to these stories.

We are three women with three perspectives on a place that, like its people, is constantly changing. That is never still.

* roosts - fierce conflicting currents around the Isle
noosts - stone-lined hollows the boats were sheltered in when out of the water
yoals - boats
yowes - ewes
kishies - open 'backpack' made of woven straw
krubs - stone walled enclosures for starting kale
baas - sunken rocks only seen when the tide is low
geos - steep-sided inlets
kletts - flat rocks formed in horizontal layers, traditionally used by courting couples to get some privacy
voar - spring planting-time
hairst - autumn harvesting

Note on Fair Isle dialect
In the Archipelago known as Shetland, variations in dialect are numerous and diverse. Fair Isle has its own particularly distinctive way with words, hence the differences in spelling and pronunciation from many of the other areas in Shetland where dialect can still be heard.

Bios:

Joan Lennon
Part thistle, part maple leaf. Joan came to Scotland from Canada in 1978 to work at the Abbey on Iona, another small island. A move to Fife, a PhD, four sons, careers in music teaching, writing and mentoring, and some wonderful residencies later, she is still here and still applying.
www.joanlennon.co.uk

Anne Sinclair
Anne's Fair Isle family tree reaches back into the 17th century. Her passions include history, music, craft, ethnology, textile and clothing construction throughout the Northern Hemisphere, the state of the planet, being a granny and a greatgranny. She is a folksinger and lecturer on history and textiles at home and abroad.

Lucy Wheeler
Having grown up on Fair Isle, and now living and working in Shetland, Lucy's creative practice is inspired by the coastal environment and dramatic weather of these islands. Anne Sinclair was one of her earliest creative influences, teaching Lucy to knit and sew at Fair Isle Primary School, introducing her to a love of texture and colour which continues to influence her art today.
www.lucywheelerart.co.uk

13

Interlaef

Nivver noticed,
de laund oagit nort,
an auld auld vaige
fae neebin blue green suddrin sea

te whaur
de wind snikkit sautbrak
fae de grøy skröf – nyivlin
at it in its jaas an spittin it oot

til
quoyd in ice white miles -
grippit deep inunder
nivver seen, de laund wis grindin inte shaeps

til
whin dat leng bittersie haed aesed -
bergs kuglin inte bumlie seas -
whin de whaul gits flowed ageen

boats kem ahint

Interleave

Unobserved,
the land crept north,
an ancient centimetric journey
from sleepy turquoise southern seas

to where
the wind snatched spray
from off slate waves – worrying
at it in its jaws and spitting it away

until
stilled in ice white miles -
gripped while deep beneath
unseen, the land was grinding into shapes

until
when that long freeze had eased -
bergs toppling into bulging seas -
when the whale roads flowed again

ships followed

Wen

Døy an nytht
shü heard de roarin fae de løybrak.
'Listen!' her man had saed.
'Hit's jüst lik de wind yealdrin i de treetaps.
Hit's jüst lik a gowster i de forest.'

Shü nodded, though it wisna true.
Hit wisna lik dat. Hit wis an uncan yealdrin, fae an uncan craig.
Hit meed a fül o her.
It haed nøy teels te tael her.
It haed nøy teels fur her te tael.

Dey haed launded a'a gale
been büld a'a gale
an in de døys an nythts
dey wottid fur de fury te aese

dey haed spüred her fur teels
sengs
bit shü haed neen.

Shü haed spewed aa her wirds
owwer de gunnel
(trailin ahint dem,
did de fysh dat glipit
her spewins
sweem doun among de leng waur
an winder?)

One

Day and night
she heard the roaring from the shore.
'Listen!' her man had said.
'It's just like the wind shouting in the treetops.
It's just like a storm in the forest.'

She nodded, even though it wasn't true.
It wasn't like that.
It was a different roaring, from a different throat.
It mocked her.
It had no stories to tell her.
It had no stories for her to tell.

They had landed in the gale
been gathered in to shelter in the gale
and in the days and nights
they waited for the fury to pass

they had asked her for stories
songs
but she had none.

She had vomited all her words
over the side of the boat,
(trailing behind them,
did the fish who ate
her sick
swim down amongst the tall kelp fronds
and think strange thoughts?)

Shü haed kent de speereets dat baed a'a trees,
de forest eens.
Shü haed tauld der teels and sung der sengs
aroond de herdsteen i de leng dark nythts.

Bit here, der wis nøy trees

de rocks wir unkan
an even de sea wisna de sem.

At heem, shü kud see de idder side o de fjord
an de deep green pines grippin de moontin.

Here, der wis nøy idder side

jüst a bummlie grøy line
whaur de grøy o de watter rekkit up te meet
de grøy o de lift

an den baith turned black
an der wis aunly de soond o de white watter
hammerin an dreggin on de black kletts

Der Finn haed deied at winter's aend
An, fae den,
'We'd dün wir best
te ant de saesons
lik dey wir wint te be
an keepit de rytht wye.
We paat oot what we cud
fur de Güdfikks ...'

She had known the spirits that lived in the trees,
the forest people.
She had told their stories and sung their songs
around the fire in the long winter nights.

But here, there were no trees

the rocks were different
and even the sea was not the same.

At home, she could see the other side of the fjord
and the deep green pines clinging to the mountain.

Here, there was no other side

only a heaving grey line
where the grey of the water reared up to meet
the grey of the sky

and then both turned black
and there was only the sound of the white waves
pounding and dragging at the black shore.

Their Finn had died at winter's end
and, since then,
'We've done our best
to keep the timings
as they're meant to be
and things kept properly.
We put out what we could
for the good folk …'

Dey seemed te want te plaes
an, keepin true, te shaw dat dey
haid been weel shawn

'...an nu de koo haed cauved
a lüm o mylk be de door ...?'

Dey crooded roond her.
Der smael wis unkan,
chokkin.

De peerie eens
oagin closser
as if dat mytht taeze a teel
oot o her
taeze a seng.
Shü tried te smile
til der midders geddered dem awa.

Dey lukkit at een anidder
glyed.
Shü heard der neesters
soondin trow
de soleed waa o wind
til, ootmeggit,
shü dwammed ower
an time güd on.

Shü maust a -
it maust a -
fur
de swit on her boady

They seemed to want to please
and, in loyalty, to show that they
had been well taught

'... and now the cow has calved,
a bowl of milk by the door ...?'

They crowded her.
Their smell was wrong
and caught in her throat.

The small ones
kept creeping close
as if that might tease a story
out of her
tease a song.
She tried to smile
until their mothers drew them away.

They looked at each other
out of the corner of their eyes.
She heard the hiss of whispering
sibilance threading through
the wall of wind roaring
until, battered,
she slept
and time passed.

She must have -
it must have -
because
the sweat on her body

wis new
an de quoyd soonded in her lug
while, inside her heed
de storm still raged
flingin her fae side te side
so dat shü mytht trip inte
de smoared fire
or staund upo de snoring, sleepin boadies
on de aert flür
bit didna.

Shü wen ta door
crakkit it aupen

an oot inte de nytht,
pechin,
grippit be de meemrie o yokkin ahed
o de coorse twistin o a towe,
kugglin ower,
bjokin,
yokkin at de coorse lubba

til shü fael still.

Aside her fiss der wis
a tin skin o ice
whaur de rain haed geddered – nøy
wind riffled de girse.

Shü felt points o somethin cauld an white
something quoyd

was new
and silence pounded her outer ear
while within her head
the storm still raged
flinging her from side to side
so that she might have stumbled into
the smoored fire
or trampled the snoring, sleeping bodies
on the earth floor
but didn't.

Instead she gained the door
heaving it ajar

and out into the night,
gasping for breath,
gripped by the memory of clutching
at the rough braiding of a rope,
falling forward,
retching,
clutching at the rough dry winter grass

until the spasm stilled.

By her face there was
a thin skin of ice
where the rain had pooled – no
wind ruffled the grass.

She felt points of something cold and white
something silent

pierce her fae abün
an when shü whummled ontae her rigg
daer wis a sky o staurs
søy stark -
tritnin -
der hertless glower
meed her coor
an sprech
an cover her fiss
wi her hauns

myndin

fu, at heem, de moontins haeld de sky
an de forest splintered de staurlytht
atween de needles an de swøy o branches ...

a kloor o claw on steen
browt her tae her feet

te fin
münlytht haed saffened de staurs
an teen her shaeda
veeve ower de aert
ower te whaur
de Güdfikk lappit
fae de lüm
be de door

heddin sae

seemin her

pierce her from above
and when she rolled onto her back
there was a sky of stars
so stark -
relentless -
their heartless stare
made her flinch
and cry out
and cover her face
with her hands

remembering

how, at home, the mountains framed the sky
and the forest splintered the starlight
between the needles and the sway of branches ...

A scuff of claw on stone
brought her to her feet

to find
moonrise had softened the stars
and brought her shadow
sharp across the ground
across to where
the trow lapped
from the bowl
by the door

pausing

acknowledging her

wi a roond e'ed blink

an turned back te feenishin
de mylk.

Den, de last slaever
ketched be her black pointy tongue,
de Güdfikk
stüd.
Her prummiks hingin
bare a'a cauld
an her belly swelled.
Shü laid a leng clawed haund
protectin
ower it, de muvment
eart kent
heddin tae hersael.

De Güdfikk grunted a wird.
Sing.
An ageen.
Sing

'I kinna.'

Sing!

'A'm lost me wirds.'

Laern new eens.

'I dünna want tae.'

with a saucer-eyed blink

and returned to finishing
the milk.

Then, the last dribble
caught with her black pointed tongue
the trow
stood.
Her breasts hung
uncovered in the cold
and her belly was swollen.
She laid a long-clawed hand
protective
across it, the gesture
familiar
possessive.

The trow grunted a word.
Sing.
And again.
Sing.

'I can't.'

Sing!

'I've lost my words.'

Learn new words.

'I ... don't want to.'

De Güdfikk lifted her shooders.
Turned roond te set aaff.

'No! wot!'

Lukkin back,
de münlytht glansin
in her roond black een.

'I dünna kaen fu.'

De Güdfikk rekkit oot wen clawed tøy,
trivvled de aedge o her shaeda.

Start afore wirds.

'A lullaby.'

A'll sing wi dee.

An in de münlytht,
past de sufferin o hert an trott,
de new seng wis boarn.

The trow shrugged.
Turned to go.

'No! Wait!'

Looking back,
the moonlight glinted
in her round black eyes.

'I don't know how.'

The trow reached out one clawed toe,
delicately touched her shadow's edge.

Begin before words.

'A lullaby.'

I will sing with you.

And in the moonlight,
past the rawness of heart and throat,
the new song began.

Interlaef

An if ivry vaige bak an fore
left sheenin gitts
lik distreen's snails
on brigsteens
or staurs' oagin roond
furnenst de black
den
de laund wid shün git
herd te scrime
in de middle o seek glow an glansin
de quoyd middle o de pinwheel's spinnin
treeds fennin oot ower de fraem
an loopin back ageen
lik solar flares
or a sunlit smeegin hund shakkin
watter draps dat flee an arc
glisterin trow de air
afore dat bördly sloo
back

Interleave

And if each voyage to and from
left luminous trails
like last night's snails
on paving stones
or stars' slow-motioned wheeling
against the black
then
the land would very soon become
impossible to see
amidst such wreathing glow and glare
the still centre of the pinwheel's spinning
lines fanning out across the wide world's seas
and looping back again
like solar flares
or a sunlit smiling dog shaking
water drops that fly and arc
glittering through the air
before that irresistible turning
returning

Twa

'Tak paece.
Du kaens fu tired du got
at de beginnin.'

I' de mirk o de howld,
her sister-in-laa grippit her airm.
'Dünna tael him,' shü saed.
'Du saed du widna tael him.'
'I winna, I saed dat. Be de time he haes te kaen,
we'll be ower fer on wir wy.
Dey'll be nøy gyaun aboot.'

Shü'd muvved in wi dem te help
wi der lippind peerie wen.
Anidder wife kem wi
anidder twau hauns
anidder streng rigg.
Bit dey'd left twa peerie moots ahint
a'a kirkyaurd
an if her bridder kent
his wife wis lippnin
he'd a whet aboot it -
it wid a teen neest te nithin
fur him te cheenge
his mind
an day widda bidden heem
keepin
brakkin heart
an rigg,

Two

'Rest now.
You know how tired you get
at the beginning.'

In the murk of the hold,
her sister-in-law clutched her arm.
'Don't tell him,' she said.
'You said you wouldn't tell him.'
'I won't. I said so. By the time he has to know,
we'll all be too far on our way.
There'll be no turning back.'

She'd moved in with them to help
with their expected family.
A spare woman brought
another pair of hands
another strong back.
But they had left two babes behind
in the kirkyard
and if her brother knew
his woman was starting another
he'd have called the great adventure off –
less than a feather's weight would have done that –
would have turned the scales
of his resolve
and they would all have stayed,
all gone on
breaking heart
and back,

hoop spleetin doon trow de years.

He musna kaen.
No yit.

'Rest nu. A'm goin abün.'
Der wis nøy answer.
Shü'd neebit ower.

Her bridder wis at de rail
an dey stüd a start
watchin de mad-eyed solans
needle beakit shooin lift te løybrak
plunge inte de middle o each white rose
an rise to sleek an fauld ageen.

Whin he axt efter his wife,
shü tauld him shü wis below,
no feelin weel.

'We'll be goin by de Isle shün.
Can du no gie her somethin?'

(Shü mytht be fey,
bit fok nivver whet comin te her
fur answers te de questions
life kem up wi.
Shü kent de plants an de herbs
an, it mytht be,
møyr.)

Shü shook her heed.
'Der's nøy hurry,' shü saed.

hope subdividing down the years.

He mustn't know.
Not yet.

'Rest now. I'm going on the deck.'
There was no answer.
She had dropped already into sleep.

Her brother was at the railing
and they stood a while
to watch the mad-eyed gannets
needle-beaked stitching sky to sea
plunge into the centre of each white rose
and rise to sleek and fold again.

When he asked for his wife,
she told him she was below,
a touch unwell.

'We'll be passing the Isle soon.
Can't you give her something?'

(She might be strange,
but it didn't stop folk coming to her
for answers to the questions
life threw.
She knew the plants and herbs
and, it might be,
more.)

She shook her head.
'There's no rush,' she said.

'A lok møyr døys an nythts
te fin sea leegs.'

Furby, de sailors haed meed it clear
de less dey saw o weemin abün daek
de better dey likkit it.
'Cauld iron' mytht turn ill luck
t'a side,
bit hit kud aunly geen søy faerr.

De barque, as weel, dat wis takkin dem awa
kud aunly geen is faerr is barques kud
an dey wir goin faerder dan dat.

Dey wir goin tae a sister
deep inlaund
in de new woerld.

'Dey hae a hunder kinds o tree,'
shü wrat,
'bit aunly wen wird fur wave.'

A maw sweeled aside de barque a start,
peerie faeders liftin
lytht aleng wing taps, winderin,
den slooed awa
heedin fur de mark on de horizon
dat wis heem.

Shü pat her haund inte her pooch
an haeld herd te de peerie steen shü'd gedderd
fae de shoormal.

'Plenty more days and nights
to find sea legs.'

Besides, the sailors had made it clear
the less they saw of women on their deck
the better they'd like it.
'Cold iron' might turn the edge
of ill luck,
but it could only go so far.

The ship, too, that was taking them away
could only go as far as ships could
and they were going further than that.

They were going to a sister
deep inland
in the new world.

'They have a hundred types of tree,'
she wrote,
'but only one word for wave.'

A gull glided level with the ship a while,
small feathers lifting
light along wing tops, inquisitive,
then peeled away
towards the smudge on the horizon
that was home.

She dug her hand into her pocket
and held hard to the pebble she had picked up
from the shore.

Der sister haed writtin te warn dem,
'Dey oanly knap whaur we bide.'

Nøy roosts, noosts
yoals an yows
kishies an krubs
baas, geos an kletts

nøy voar an hairst.

Wid dey tink her bakaboot,
de wye shü spak streenge
brokken up be aw de mants
peerie bit perceptible
as her heed reckit fur wirds
dat kem second te what shü toitht?
Bit mibbe better backaboot dan oorie.

Nøybody saed it.
Nøybody wis søyin,
'In de new pliss,
dünna be unkan.'
Bit shü kent hit wis on aubody's mind.

So mony wyes o bein unkan.
Wioot tinkin, shü seemed te faw
inte ivvry wen.
Sittin ootside be hersael
in de nytht.
Sweemin trow de mareel,
blue lytht drippin føy her white limbs.

Their sister had written to warn them,
'It's only the English they speak here.'

No roosts, noosts
yoals and yows
kishies and krubs
baas, geos and kletts

no voar and hairst.

Would she seem slow and dim,
her speaking awkward
paced with all the pauses
tiny but perceptible
as her head reached for words
that were second to the words that came?
But maybe better dim than strange.

No one was saying it.
No one was saying,
'In the new place,
don't be strange.'
But she knew it was in everyone's mind.

So many ways of being strange.
Without effort, she'd seemed to fall
into them all.
Sitting alone outside
in the night.
Swimming in the mareel,
blue light dripping from her white limbs.

Singin te de staurs
lik de Güdfikks.
Plaesed te drittle
saft-fitted
trow ask an fug,
shü mytht a been a gamfer.
Kaenin things ...

Der mytht be a man fur her
in dis new woerld
Nøybody wis søyin it.
Nøybody wis søyin,
'Mebbe if shü mairies whik -
afore dey fin oot ower mukkle -
hit mytht be aurytht.'
Bit shü kent dey wir aw tinkin dat.

(Ivryeen's business
wis ivryeen's business,
an an unmairied wife, møyr dan mist.)

Closser ta'a laund, waves cheenged
shaep an smail an speed.
'De moder dy,' saed her bridder,
an geed te staund wi de idder men.

Closser, de Isle cheenged
fae smudge te shaep.
An ootline.
A soleed lump.
o lent an hytht

Singing to the stars
like a trow.
Walking willingly
so soft-footed
through mist and fog,
she might have been a gamfer.
Knowing things ...

Maybe there'd be a husband for her,
in this new world.
No one was saying it.
No one was saying,
'Maybe if she marries quick -
before they find too much out -
maybe it'll be all right.'
But she knew it was on everyone's mind.

(Everyone's business
was everyone's business,
and a spinster, more than most.)

Closer to land, waves changed
shape and smell and speed.
'The moder dy,' said her brother,
and went to stand with the other men.

Closer to, the Isle had changed
from smudge to shape.
A silhouette.
A bulk.
A length and height

no mizzered be fitsteps
bit be ee.

Her sytht wis leng.

Mebbe dat wis why
dey'd stowed her hosiery
at de bodam o de bundle
te be bartered.
Mebbe dat wis why her pautrens
wir sometimes kinda unkan.
Wen geeng o colour
oot a traep.

Bit even wi her leng sytht,
even is de Isle oagit closs,
shü kuddna see
de lukki minnie's oo -
banks flooers, büld a'a girse -
de wy sheep gitts fenned oot
veeve trow de dry haeder
an mallimunks flew der shaedas
ower de fiss o de banks
an de laund
wis rippled wi rigs
up te de hill dikk.

Shü kuddna see dem
bit shü kent dey wir dere.

not measured by footstep
but by eye.

Her sight was long.

Maybe that was why
they put her knitting
at the bottom of the bundle
to be bartered.
Maybe that was why her patterns
were sometimes a touch odd.
One line of colour
out of the order.

But even with her long sight,
even as the Isle crept close,
she couldn't see
the bog cotton flying their flags of fluff -
pinks, snugged down tight amongst the grasses -
the way the sheep tracks rayed out
beige through the brittle heather
and fulmars flew their shadows
across the cliff face
and the land
was rippled by rigs
up to the hill dyke.

She couldn't see them
but she knew they were there.

An fur a start,
though shü kent de barque wis muvin,
hit wis lik shü wis staundin still
as de shaep o de Isle oagit slowly
slowly
by.

De Niz an Mopul
Wirvie an Restensgeo
Buness
Finniquoy
Goorn
Sheep Craig an Klinger's Geo
De Rippack
De Breks
De Burrian
De Baa Green
Meoness an Kirkigeo
De Keels an De Skerry ...

Hit wis de rissenin glister
aff de waater
meed dem blur.
Saut tears fael doon
inte saut sea.
Shü tisted daem
mixed wi de saut mist
on her lips.

And for a time,
though she knew the ship was moving,
it seemed that she was standing still
as the shape of the Isle scrolled slowly
slowly
by.

De Niz and Mopul
Wirvie and Restensgeo
Buness
Finniquoy
Goorn
Sheep Craig and Klinger's Geo
De Rippack
De Breks
De Burrian
De Baa Green
Meoness and Kirkigeo
De Keels and De Skerry ...

It was the diamond glitter
off the water
made them blur.
Salt tears fell down
into salt sea.
She tasted them
mingled with the salt mist
on her lips.

Shü laid de plisses doon
ahint her een
stored dem
wi her unkanness -

dey'd been tauld te traivel lytht -

an turned her leng sytht
inte de future,

kaenin things ...

kaenin dat de peerie sowel
startin te form i de dark below
wid live
wid be boarn
inte dis mukkle adventure
wid be wen
te unpack fur.

She laid the places down
behind her eyes
stored them
with her strangeness -

they'd been told to travel light -

and turned her long sight
to the future,

knowing things ...

knowing that the child
beginning in the dark below
would live
would be born
into the great adventure
would be one
to unpack for.

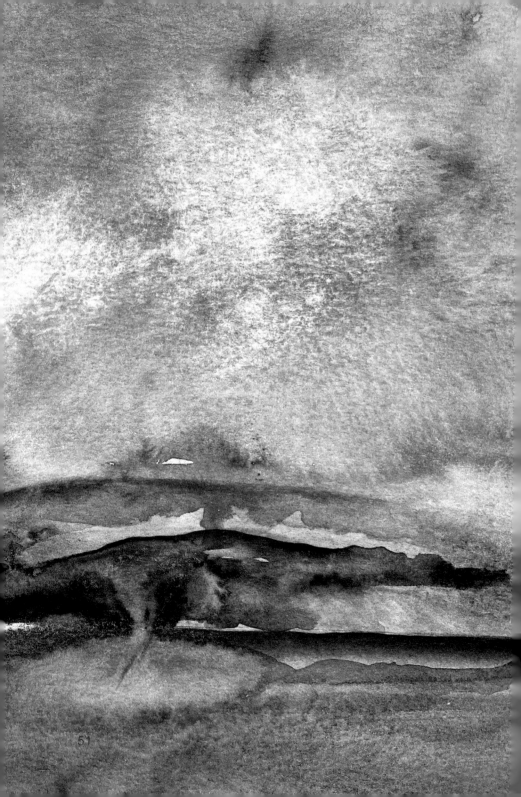

Interlaef

trow time,
de middle o de aert slippit sooth
an de laund baed
a'a box
on de map
in a coarner
dat nøy idder body wis üsin

while de auld ice
shrukkin
steered tegidder
greetin
its fraeshness
inte de saut sea

an still onlyin
nivver leetin maps
tides wrat ageen
oot a sytht yit veeve
te be raed
be de fugle
sweelin

an geos filt
lost der waus te waves
is de watter kem up
lippit past fences
oaged alleng gitts
lippered ower brigsteens

Interleave

in time,
the centre of the world slipped south
and the land lived
in a box
on the map
in a corner
that no one else was using

while the old ice
dwindled
mingled
weeping
its freshness
into the salt sea

and surging all
unencumbered by cartography
gyre-rewritten
invisible yet clear
to be read
by seabirds
under glide

and geos filled
lost their walls to waves
as the water rose
lipped past fences
crept along the roads
lapped over door sills

de shaeda o orca
slid ower de grave steens
an de lyththoose braethd saut
in an oot
whaur de gless haed been
whaur de lytht haed pittin hits sharp baet
o brytht and aese
inte de hert o de nyth

treeless laand
owergeen bi waur

hedfasted aishins doon,
inunder traeshin drooie lines

wave mirl, bufferin
de rock still in air

the shadows of orca
slid across the graveyard
and the lighthouse breathed sea salt
in and out
where the glass had been
where the light had sent its rhythmic stab
of bright and pause
into the heart of the dark

treeless land
whelmed and forested by kelp

holdfasts storeys down
under fronds' thrash and flail

wave maze, buffering
the rock still in air

Tree

Shü'd come ashore
on Meennie's Heed
a'a high white sun
an a skirl o tirricks.

Der haed been damage
fae de gowster.
Stipes haed snapped.
Rocks rowled
haed rummled up de aeb.
Anchorhaeld tang slippit
lik stubby fingers.
Froands laid flat an wupitt
flatched oot be wytht o air

de wytht o air -
shü felt tü
bumlin ower de shoormal
te fin her feet
on aert an haeder
a tin skin
ower steen

up on de slopp
te whaur de bruks o de lukoot biggins
brukkit withoot a soond

an stüd a start

te wotch de maws wide-winged
birl an yall

Three

She'd come ashore
on Minnie's Head
in a high white sun
and a skirl of terns.

There'd been damage
from the storm.
Stipes had snapped.
Rocks rolled
had tumbled up the shoreline.
Holdfast stumps unclasped
like stubby fingers.
Fronds laid flat and tangled
splayed out by weight of air

the weight of air -
she felt it too
stumbling across the foreshore
to find her feet
on turf and heather
a thin skin
over stone

on up the slope
to where the ruined lookout buildings
crumbled quietly

and stood a while

to watch the gulls wide-winged
wheel and yell

de scarfs sun-worship
on de stack

trak staedy whauls
de smooth curve o riggs vaigin
de tooers o spume
dat lift an drift t'a side

Den wipe de saut fae de poower panels
an read de gauges -
heliograph, pyranometer,
anemometer, barometer.

Since afore shü wis boarn,
hit wis ower lit te whyte de cheenge
an de wye backlins still a piece te geen
an heddin søy

fraeshnin de air
a liff at a time
an whaur der wis nøy laund
fur laeves,
forests a'a seas
haulin in ower mony
haundfastit atoms
i da air aboot wis
inte ocean,
hoidin a'a waur's
broon froands,
hoidit an hüld
in de hoop o healin.

the shags sun-worship
on the stack

track steady whales
the smooth curving of backs progressing
the columns of spume
that lift and drift aside

Then wipe the salt from the power panels
and read the gauges -
heliograph, pyranometer,
anemometer, barometer.

Since before she was born,
it was too late to stop the change
and the journey back still long
and patient

refreshing the air
a leaf at a time
and where there was no land
for leaves,
forests in the seas
drawing those too many
bonded atoms
from atmosphere
into ocean,
sequestered in the kelp's
bronze fronds,
hidden and held
in the hope of healing.

Dey caud her de warden
an, if a boat wis passin,
dey kem wi whativver
she kuddna geddir
fae de laundskip dat wis laund nøy lenger
her sprawlin underwatter toon.

Shü likkit de auld neems
so shü caud de waur
her croft -
her rig -
hers te mind, her maet-press.

Readins raed, shü kem back ta'a sea.
(De gowster haed kept her on de land
fur twartree døys
an nu, slippit
kem te patrol, tink,
an winder.)

Shü wis at heem a'a watter
an when de sylkies kem te dance an sweel
winderin atween de muvin stipes,
shü mirrored dir sooplnis
wi anserin aese
til dey skeeted ta'a side
an shü güd on.

Shü haed been geen a heedlamp
though shü furjat maest days
te tak it wi her -

They called her the warden
and, if a boat was passing,
they kept her in whatever
she couldn't get
from the landscape that was no longer land
her sprawling underwave demesne.

She liked the old names
so she called the kelp
her croft -
her park -
it was her stewardship and larder.

Readings read, she came back to the sea.
(The storm had kept her on the land
these last few days
and now, release
returned her to patrol, assess,
consider.)

She was at home in the water
and when seals came to twine and wreath
curious between the swaying stipes,
she mirrored their effortlessness
with answering ease
until they flashed aside
and she went on.

She'd been given a head-lamp
though she forgot most days
to bring it -

dark een skrymin a'a dim lytht
doon te de rocks an wrakks.

Dey meed her vexed te begin wi

so mony brukit beens o boats
on dat 'most unpitying' coast
de ful circle o whaat de Isle haed been,
girt, year upo year
wi teels nu leng lost whaur kent
an mony nivver kent
te tael

til de wrakks turned inte
de beens o reefs explodin
wi staurfysh, blüd reed anemone
shag-rug sea-slug an waivin weed
dat set de ooter aeges o her tunship.

Dey haed teen de brunt o de gowster
bit fur nu
shü geed efter,
nivver seen,
a sheenin blinnd hoe nort
(boarn fae a purse
slaed oot atween de hoarns
inta de nursery
o froands)
nort aleng whaur de auld gitt løy.

dark eyes served in the gloom
down to the rocks and the wrecks.

They had made her sad at first

so many craft who broke their bones
on that 'most unpitying' coast,
the full circle of what the isle had been,
girt, year after year,
with stories now long lost where known
and many never known
to tell

until the wrecks became
the bones of reefs rich blossoming
with brittlestar, blood red anemone,
shag-rug sea-slug and waving weed
that marked the furthest boundaries of her world.

They'd have taken the brunt of the storm
but for now
she followed,
unobserved,
a silver dog fish north
(born from a purse
slithered out between the horns
into a nursery
in the fronds)
north along where the old road lay.

On auld shaedas o waus
krubs
boondri lines
dat metched inte de boddam's
drooned shaeps,
markit withoot bleem
geddirin piltiks an creb
lobster an silliks
an flukkerin gyuddikks

der safe heem.

Nu an den aleng de wy
shü wid dive deep
an triss de helt o
hedfast
stipe
blaeders
an froands
wen among de mony
an wis content.

De kelp got peerier is de slopp aesed
draain up on anidder shore
til shü wis ta'a hochs ageen
an felt de chill o de wind
a'a hümin.

Shü followed de burn
up Warden's Hill,
bidin a peerie start whar de watter ran fraesh

On past suggestions of walls
enclosures
demarcations
that blended with the seafloor's
drowned topography,
texturing without rancour
accommodating saithe and crab
lobster and fingerlings
and flickering sandeel

unquestioned tenancy.

From time to time along the way
she would pause
to trace the health of
holdfast
stipe
bladders
and fronds
of one among the many
and was content.

The kelp shortened as the gradient eased
towards another shore
till she was knee-deep again
and felt the chill of the wind
at day's end.

She followed the stream
up Warden's Hill,
pausing where the water ran fresh

back fae de saut tide
an watched de dratsies dook an trig
mirlin i der saut-freed fur.

'Güd wark de døy,' shü tauld dem.

(Lengin fur skedmans heeds'
juicy middles,
der hairsts coosed
her forests hedfasts -
ivry giant's
anchor-
ivry giant's
waekness.)

Ower wen soople shouder
a peerie flyt.
Hit wis just fur shaw.
Dey wir wint wi her.

Shü fen her stride,
buksed on
while ahint her,
Sheep Craig lost de aend
o de lytht,
dippit inte de mirknin.

Hit maust hi been
pikkit clean
afore her time
bit de tap o Warden's Hill wis still trussit,
still kleggit wi bits o machine,

back from the tide brine
and watched the otters bath and groom
ecstatic in their salt-freed fur.

'Good work today,' she told them.

(Insatiable for sea urchins'
succulent centres,
their harvests saved
her forest's holdfasts -
each giant's
anchor -
each giant's
Achilles' heel.)

Over one supple shoulder,
a perfunctory scold.
It was just for show.
They were used to her.

She found her stride,
climbed on
while behind her,
Sheep Rock lost the last
of the light,
dipped into darkness.

It must have been
picked clean
before her time
but the top of Warden's Hill was still strewn,
still lumped with pieces of machine,

trawn ingines
roogin
roosted üsliss;
concrete steps
leadin nøywy;
splintered shaeps
nøy lenger
fainin
te come at.

Shü'd lat dem lie

an meed her bül
in a gyll
haff-gitts ta'a tap
whaur de rain gaederd in a whampi
an lik de dratsies
shü cud rinse de seasaut
føy her høyr,
lat what wis fraish mind her skin
o idder wys

an whin shü shiggled free,
de mirri dancers shawd, a half circle
at de boddam o de lift,
a glansin a'a nort.

'I raed fu toons üsed te dü just dat,'
shü saed tae nøy een
is shü sat on de brigsteen
an combed de wirds fae her høyr.

stubborn engines
rearing up
rusted beyond name;
concrete steps
leading nowhere;
splintered structures
no longer speaking
to any purpose,
pursuant to any plan.

She'd let them lie

and made her shelter
in a hollow
halfway up
where the rain filled the lochan
and, like the otters,
she could rinse the seasalt
from her hair,
let what was fresh remind her skin
of other ways

and when she shook free,
the Aurora showed, a semi-circle
at the bottom of the sky,
a glow in the north.

'I read how cities used to do just that,'
she said to no one
as she sat on her doorstep
and combed the words from her hair.

'Dey cud be miles awa,
rytht ower de horizon,
bit dey wid lytht de sky up
jüst lik dat,' shü saed
an güd in trow.

Fur hit wis time
te løy doon de døy,
løy doon de beens athin her skin,
an coose de roond horizon
inte dreams
dat swem an sweeled
wir nivver still.

An in de high stutter o de sky,
de sun's flaans ruckled
aert's coloured courteens o lytht
an meed dem reel.

'They could be miles away,
right over the horizon,
but they would light the sky up
just like that,' she said
and went inside.

For it was time
to lay down the day,
lay down the bones within her skin,
and wrap the round horizon
into dreams
that swam and span,
were never still.

And in the high stutter of the sky,
the sun's winds ruckled
earth's coloured curtains of light
and made them dance.

Interlaef

an løybrak brook on banks
on banks
on banks
aesin shaeps
ooto whaat seemed aert-fast

while drittlin shoals o staurs
swem de mün's high rod,
vimmerin inunder
de brodd brimmin
braethin sea

Interleave

and waves broke against rock
against rock
against rock
easing shapes
out of what seemed adamant

while slow shoals of stars
swam the moon's high road,
spangling below
the wide encircling
breathing sea